Taurus

THIS BOOK BELONGS TO:

_____

THE WONDERFUL WORLD OF ZODIACS

TAURUS

Mimi Jones

Dedicated to my grandson Joey.

All rights reserved.
No part of this book may be reproduced in any form or by any means, electronic or mechanical, and no photocopying or recording, unless you have written permission from the author.

ISBN 978-1-958985-48-9

Text copyright © 2025 by Mimi Jones

www.joeysavestheday.com

A Mimi Book

THE WONDERFUL WORLD OF ZODIACS

TAURUS

Mimi Jones

Dates:

Taurus spans from April 20 to May 20.

Ruling Planet:

Venus rules Taurus.

Personality:

Taureans are known for being reliable and patient.

STUBBORN

Weakness:
Taureans can be stubborn and possessive.

TAURUS

Color:

Their lucky colors are green and pink.

Taurus

Lucky Numbers:

2, 6, 9, and 12 are lucky for Taureans.

Compatibility:

Taurus gets along well with Cancer, Virgo, Capricorn, and Pisces.

CANCER

VIRGO

CAPRICORN

PISCES

Dislikes:

They dislike sudden changes and complications.

Likes:

Taureans love stability, luxury, and nature.

Taurus

Career:

They excel in careers that require practicality and determination.

Positive Trait:

Taureans are very loyal and reliable.

Negative Trait:

Sometimes, they can be too indulgent and resistant to change.

Taurus

Motto:

Their motto is "I have."

Favorite Day:

Wednesday and Friday are their favorite days.

wednesday

&

FRIDAY

Health:

Taureans should take care of their throat and neck.

take care

take care

Take Care of Yourself

Challenges:

Taureans need to learn to embrace flexibility and adaptability.

Taurus

Friendship:

They are dependable friends who will always be there for you.

Influence:

They inspire others with their steadfastness and reliability.

TAURUS

Favorite Activities:

Taureans love activities that involve nature and relaxation.

If this Zodiac gem tickled your celestial fancy, then you're in for a treat! Dive into my other Zodiac delights right here:

www.mimibooks.com

THE END!

www.ingramcontent.com/pod-product-compliance
Lightning Source LLC
Chambersburg PA
CBHW040030050426
42453CB00002B/70